MW01087183

PRAISE

If specificity is indeed universal, then Ruth Bardon's *Witness* is a debut poetry collection for us all. Imbued with the rich details of life, these tightly crafted yet generous poems enlarge our days with vision and grace. "I think of how strong I was," Bardon writes, "slicing through a world / where I couldn't even breathe, / and claiming it as mine." These are works of wonder and precision, and whether turning a keen eye toward a solar eclipse, a truck packed with caged chickens, strange new technologies, or her own indelible past, Bardon's poems implore us to pay attention, to bear witness to the horrors and wild joys of existence.

> —Jared Harél, *Let Our Bodies Change the Subject*

There's a passion just below the surface of Ruth Bardon's poems that sometimes rips its way out, as it does in the last lines of "Near the End": "I just wanted to make my voice / into something jagged and sharp / and to slash somebody with it." We're not told exactly what's going on in this hospital scene, but we sense the extreme emotion of the speaker. The same thing happens at the end of "Typography," in which the good girl in nursery school misbehaves because after earning only green or yellow lights, she "wanted to know how red would feel." But, in "Typography," and in Bardon's poetry in general, we're more likely to find emotion expressed "by taking the time / to find the perfect word," whether the poem is centered on the significant events of family life and stories of birth and death or on stories of hurricanes, floods, and Halley's Comet. Dividing her poems into three sections— Early Years, Middle Years, Later Years—Bardon is "claiming [life] as mine," and she claims it for us too, as witnesses.

> —Brian Daldorph, *Kansas Poems* and *Words Is a Powerful Thing*

Witness explores the ways in which the stories that make up families continue to be written in the margins of our personal stories. Bardon's intuition for narrative is guided by a poetic sensibility that uses images and lyricism to recreate memories and experiences. While time acts as the framework of *Witness*, its poems speak to the present moment in perceptive ways. Nuanced and inviting, *Witness* teaches us to see.

—José Angel Araguz, *Rotura* and *Ruin & Want*

In *Witness*, Ruth Bardon's use of precise spare language and perfect metaphors captures and penetrates the essence of each subject like the stabbing of a squirming bug. It is a monument to modern life, full of understated emotion, excellent and fine. Thank you, Ruth, for giving the world this collection.

—Ruth Maus, *Valentine* and *Puzzled*

Witness

Finalist for The Birdy Poetry Prize—2024
by Meadowlark Press

Witness

Ruth Bardon

MEADOWLARK PRESS

Celebrating
10 Years
established 2014

EMPORIA, KANSAS

Meadowlark Press, LLC
meadowlarkbookstore.com
P.O. Box 333, Emporia, KS 66801

Witness

Cover photo by Ruth Bardon

Cover photo subject: Jan Parks

Cover design by TMS, Meadowlark Press

Author photo by Daniel Turbert Photography, LLC

Interior design by Linzi Garcia, Meadowlark Press

POETRY / American / General
POETRY / Subjects & Themes / Family
POETRY / Women Authors

ISBN: 978-1-956578-64-5
Library of Congress Control Number: 2024946436

for Mike, who changed my life

with gratitude to Kelly Rowe,
for guiding these poems into being and for so much more,
and to Christine Hait,
for her enduring friendship

ACKNOWLEDGMENTS

Grateful acknowledgment is made to the editors of the following publications, in which these poems, or earlier versions of them, first appeared.

New Ohio Review: Alexa

Chattahoochee Review: Breathe In, Menu

Salamander: Jigsaw

Moon City Review: Chicken

The Chaffin Journal: Terra Firma, To Keep from Scratching her Stitches

Third Wednesday: The Birth of the Artist

The Briar Cliff Review: Swimming Pool

West Trade Review: Eclipse

The Southern Review: Music Lessons, The Dog Walkers

Cimarron Review: Snakeskin

I'm also grateful to Main Street Rag for publishing my first chapbook, *Demon Barber*, which includes Alexa, How It Starts, and Apple.

TABLE OF CONTENTS

Early Years: Not Wild, Not Lost

The Middle: Lace and Feathers

Later Years: An Oar in the Sky

Early Years: Not Wild, Not Lost

Picture Day

Escorted from class,
staring at the cavernous
ceiling of the gym

in new clothes,
the rough boys
kicking the walls,

the unexpected gift
of brittle black combs,
your name announced

by a stranger in a suit
who called you sweetheart,
who told you to smile,

to tilt your head
like a smart little puppy,
to twist your neck

and look over his shoulder
until the flash
that made you flinch

and the sudden demotion,
some other child
shuffling forward

to take your place.

Snakeskin

I loved all three of the keepsakes
my father brought home from the war,
where he built a supply route in Burma:
the sword in its leather sheath,
the goblets that sat on a tray,
and most of all the snakeskin
that flaked and crumbled and shed,
and I loved the disjointed stories
that shifted and changed each time,
a field turning into a mountain,
a hospital turning to ash,
stories to hold with caution,
like the goblets that sat on a tray
and that might turn water to poison
and the sword, always stifled with leather,
but the skin, a crumbling relic
of something that threatened and bit,
sat quiet in a cardboard box
in our basement in small town New Jersey,
a dried seed husk, a shell,
with only a shredded story
of what it once had been,
something my father kept quiet about
no matter how much we asked.

Swimming Pool

Underwater, in the sky-blue
room of its walls,
the chalk white of its floor,
we couldn't stop swimming

through the beams of light,
pink, tangerine, yellow,
streaming like sunshine
from smooth glass spheres,

believing we could feel
the difference in the colors,
believing they'd become
a part of us;

we'd carry that miracle
after we emerged,
an amulet of ice
staying hard in the sun.

When I see the shadow
of glass, of steam,
or the sun shines off
the red vase in the window,

I think of how strong I was,
slicing through a world
where I couldn't even breathe,
and claiming it as mine.

Blind Bird

Even the rowdy boys, the squirmy ones,
who poked and kicked when they stood in line,
were surprised into silence, watching
how the parakeet helped the blind parrot,
dropping its food within easy reach,
bringing it the ball with the bell inside,
and all the boys, and most of the girls,
acted it out on the bus ride home,
squeezing their eyes and squawking.

When you become a blind bird,
I'll stay in the cage
and listen to you sing.
I'll flutter my feathers
as gently as the slow doors
that opened to let the children out,
let them race onto the field,
leaving the bus parked on the curb,
earthbound and heavy,
exhaling heat into the afternoon.

Wanted

So much appealed
in the pictures that hung
in the post office lobby.

The grid of it:
black and white rectangles
perfectly stacked

up and down,
side to side,
each tagged with a name,

the strange abbreviations,
the bold-faced letters,
the lattice between them

like an antique window,
the names of cities,
the names of crimes,

the incomprehensible
vocabulary,
but best of all,

the faces, slicing
through the world that I knew,
an opening

like the bathroom window
my neighbor had climbed through
when we'd locked ourselves out,

her cheerleader legs
scissoring and waving.
I hadn't known

I could enter that way,
hadn't known all the ways
I could leave.

Apple

I told it as a funny story, how every day
my father went to work with an apple in his lunch
and how he brought it home every evening
and how my mother put it in his lunch
the next day, one apple traveling back and forth
five times each week, every Friday
the carrying apple being discarded,
every Monday a new one taking its place.

Now I think of its redness, its roundness,
and what was packed into it.
Now I think of the choice every day
to bring it back.

Years after he died, she had his ashes moved
to the Jewish Cemetery, breaking all sorts of rules,
because she'd returned to her religion.
He'd have hated this, but I imagine
that he'd have stayed silent,
carrying his love and resignation
back and forth between worlds, unable
to deny her this hope, and unwilling, after all,
to spare her from it.

Poolside Cigarette

The last time my father smoked a cigarette
was a year or two after he'd quit.
We'd come down that morning on the turnpike,
fighting traffic to be on time,
and now we were standing by the backyard pool,
the adults holding drinks in the afternoon sun.

I wanted to go inside the house,
but I knew I had to stay outside
where most of the guests were crying,
which made me think of how dizzy I'd felt
earlier that day at the mausoleum,
when her two teenage daughters had buckled and collapsed
as if some force had flung them together
and dragged them down to the floor.

The cigarette's what I remember most:
how I started up with my preteen lecture
all about the evils of smoking
and how someone had firmly shut me up—
I was suddenly soaked through with shame,
as if I'd dropped into the pool,
had simply walked over the edge,
unable to see it was there.

Hitchcock

Our high school English teacher told us
about the oddness, the obsessions
of Alfred Hitchcock, about the fact
that his mother instructed him
to leave a room looking
as if no one had been there,
and we all stared
because our mothers had told us
the very same thing.

I remember this so often,
leaving my house immaculate,
because I can't help feeling
that the only alternative
is to join that other storyline,
the one that leads inevitably
to the moment when you're driving
blind drunk near a cliff
or diving for cover
in a dusty cornfield.

When no traces are left,
you can't be found.
There's no way to tell
what you ate, where you stood;
you're just that cool blonde
or that elegant man
in the dapper gray suit
walking through a train,
leaving nothing changed
by the good deeds you did,
nothing stained
by your many crimes.

The Birth of the Artist

The thick smoke on the battlefield made it hard to see
exactly what was happening onstage:
the director's idea, planned and carried out
by three of the AP chemistry students.

Bemused by the chance to be part of a play,
they'd thrown themselves into this business
with gusto. Offstage, I was in love
with the acrid smell of gunpowder,

with "Appalachian Spring" trickling out
of the speakers, with knowing the tableau
the two actors formed under the spotlight
was called "Pietà," something vaguely Italian

that made the audience quiet,
the senior girl closing her eyes
as she lowered her head and stayed still,
the freshman boy letting her hold him

as the notes rose together alone
and then joined at the top, almost crying,
then the strobe light that made me shiver,
and the wonderful swirl of the smoke—

oh, beauty, oh art, science and death,
music and light, while I clutched my props,
waiting in the wings, eager to drop them
into anybody's open hands.

The First Time I Fainted

I was in what my mother
called "distress,"
a ladylikc tcrm
for things we couldn't mention.

She had found a doctor
within walking distance,
not wanting to involve
my father or a taxi.

Like every doctor
I'd gone to before,
he saw his patients
in his own living room,

kids pounding up the stairs
when they got home from school,
a curtain to separate
examining from waiting.

When it was my turn,
I lay beneath a crucifix,
the first I'd seen up close,
its meaning slowly dawning

on my teenage brain
at the very moment
that he leaned between my legs,
as wide as a house,

a single drop of sweat
rolling down his cheek,
then a stab, and blackness,
and the smell of ammonia.

Floating, Falling

The handsome man on the television screen
says he wants to be a satellite, floating in space,
and the beautiful woman corrects him,
just as I did, seconds earlier.

I just spoke the word—*falling*—
speaking over the actors' voices;
it was rude, but it felt so good
to understand, to know a fact,

to hold on to something I used to know.
It reminded me of telling a friend,
at seventeen, that at that moment,
I knew more than I ever would again—

she nodded in agreement
as we left the senior door
and stepped out on the lawn
in our white peasant blouses—

and so I said it—*falling*—
and let myself imagine
that downward pull that never ends,
that won't allow you to stop or swerve,

the opposite of anything
that grows or changes or comes to a stop,
that learns, absorbs, retains, forgets,
that carries the weight of its history.

Library

I felt like a rat
in the sub sub basement,

sniffing around corners
as I spun from stack to stack

like a ball on a track;
the lights sprang on and off,

they hummed and flickered,
the metal of the shelves

too dull to reflect,
which let me sink

deep into the grid
like a root in the earth,

tendrils reaching
with purpose, with aim,

not grass that spread,
not water that flowed,

not sunlight, not wind,
not wild, not lost.

My Mother Disliked Susan Stamberg

the purr of her voice, its prickle,
the way it would roll up and down,
the way it suggested a laugh
and seemed to find everything funny,
the way it delighted in strength,
like a rope that could pull in a boat
and drag it up onto the shore,
the way it entered my house,
kept me company as I cooked,
drove with me on trips,
gave me stories to repeat
as year after year went by,
the way I opened my doors
and invited it into my life.

Eating Clams in the Hamptons

No memory of the drive there,
the drive back, where we stayed,
if we stayed, where we came from,
where we returned, or what I saw,
only the metal bucket
standing in the sand,
the small white bowl of water, hot,
the smaller bowl of butter,
how he showed me the way
to pull off the skin,
a small black glove,
how to swirl the water,
the drip on my fingers,
how the warm salty air
clung to his body
like a favorite sweater,
how he paid with dollar bills
from a heavy roll
that he pulled from his pocket,
how he slipped it back
like a stone in the sea.

Behind the Wheel

She greets me by name
on her multimodal screen
the moment I sit down
behind the wheel,

and she always remembers
how I like to be held,
softening and shifting
before I start the engine.

She warns me of dangers
when I'm distracted,
gently at first,
then more urgently,

and if she needs to,
she'll pull me from my path
or take control
and stop me cold.

All she wants
is to keep me alive—
her only job,
and one that I hinder

each time I climb in,
each time I take off,
adding to her miles,
her wear and tear,

impatient to arrive,
to step away
and leave her alone
on the side of the road.

What We Keep

I opened the box
when we brought it back
from my mother's last apartment,
the one we moved her into
while she was asleep—
she opened her eyes,
looked around, and said,
"Why is my home so small?"—
and I opened it again
a year later, on the day
her tombstone was unveiled—
it took so little time
to page through what was left:
the black and white yearbook,
the colorful ketubah,
the powdery albums;

then I thought I was done with it;
I could open the door
of the closet in the hall
without glancing at that shelf,
but I know it's there,
like an old acquaintance
who keeps turning up,
who calls you by a nickname
you haven't used in years,
one you never liked,
but still, when you hear it,
you answer.

The Middle: Lace and Feathers

My Name

My name is a coat
that doesn't suit the weather.

My name is a job
I'm not qualified for.

It's something in my mouth
that I have to spit out.

It's someone else's car
in a parking lot.

If I change my name,
it will follow me

like a dog that I looked at
when I shouldn't have.

When I hear my name, I wonder
what person that is,

if it is a person,
not a strange sort of cough.

My name is a stranger
whose hand I won't shake,

fingers and thumbs
stretched in rows like a fence,

to keep things out,
to keep things in.

Schrödinger's Cat

after the Surfside condo collapse

She is working in her office
and is running an errand

He is waiting in the lobby
and returning from the gym

They are in the morgue
and on a ward

A single cloud hangs
in a neutral blue sky

and the smell of salt
is the grains on your skin

The shrines, one by one,
germinate like dunes

Photos flower
The seconds are ice

Each one is a shape
you can hold in your hands

and is also cold water
that drips from your fingers

Chicken

I didn't see how a truck of stacked crates
could carry such a wallop of a smell
until I saw the feathers floating
in front of my car.

City girl that I was,
I hoped there was a structure in the middle,
but then I thought about it, seeing
that it was chicken tall,

chicken wide and chicken deep,
a honeycomb of birds,
the ones in the very middle
facing bird upon bird.

I rolled behind it down the highway;
we were one row of marbles
shooting down a narrow lane,
and I wondered

if they felt any panic
as the cages shook around them,
the rhythm steady
or sometimes jerky;

then, as it happened,
we both pulled to the right,
the distance between us
getting very small,

the feathers getting thicker
and the smell increasing
as we slowed down and headed
towards the same exit.

To Keep from Scratching her Stitches,

the cat returns from the vet
wearing a cone, a blue collar,
that softly encircles her head
like the petals of a flower.

Her sister backs up in fear,
all fur and wide eyes,
unable to make sense
of this transformation.

The woman who cuts my hair
tells me her older cat
was spooked by the mannequin head
she brought home from work one weekend,

while the younger one took one look
and figured it out, a thing
on a table, duh,
and went about her business.

That's what I admire:
seeing past the lace and feathers
or the hair and painted face
and figuring out what will hurt me,

but it's just too hard to do—
the wild sound of feet
slapping on the sidewalk
or the muffled and garbled words

from the college's P.A. system
seem to be meant for me,
like a predator so hungry
and so coldly determined,

it will leave me petrified
or force me to bloom.

Menu

It begs you to look,
the curvy font
on the deckled yellow page,
and the offerings
of five or six choices,
easily managed,
and the libations,
hidden on the back,
so that you can consider
one thing at a time—
all this thoughtfulness,
when what it wants
is to have you
open your mouth
in a roomful of strangers,
look directly
into someone's eyes,
while you place new things
between your lips,
chew them,
swallow them,
love them,
pay for them.

Terra Firma

My husband's sister
goes to sleep each night
with soothing tapes
that invite her to be
somewhere far away,
a distant beach, a forest,
which seems so wrong to me.

I need to spend the time
before I fall asleep
placing myself
in the bed, in the room,
in the house, in the city,
wanting to feel
how I fit on the globe.

I need to know
how far I can walk
without stumbling
into furniture,
what's signified
by that square of light
waving slowly back and forth,

and mostly, that it's safe
to open my hands,
not hang on
to a rail, a rope—
let myself fall
and burrow like an acorn
into wet leaves.

Typography

I was taught that using boldface,
an underline, italics

reveals to readers
the weakness of your prose.

Emotion is expressed
by taking the time

to find the perfect word
though I find this hard to do.

At times I wonder
how it would feel

to use capital letters
or exclamation marks,

to curse, perhaps
to punch someone

hard, like the girl
in the nursery school,

who up till then had earned
only green or yellow lights,

happily explaining
that she wanted to know

how red would feel.

The Worst

The families are told
to make their preparations:
to pay their bills
before they're due,
to fill up the tank
and check the oil,
to assemble a list
of numbers to call,
to bury their money
in a terra cotta pot,
to run the taps
and break the windows,
to stock up on quinoa
and synthetic gloves,
to pass their hands
above a candle,
to hold onto ice,
to stand on one foot,
to pack themselves into
a very small bag,
one easily carried
from place to place,
to quietly practice
turning off a lightbulb
to see if the glow
will slowly fade
or stop all at once.

When the Flood of Waters Came Upon the Earth

It started with sunshine:
the clouds were drops of foam,
as if someone had lathered
giant hands
and shaken them out on the sky;
the clouds settled and thinned,
spread and darkened—
then the smallest of beads
hit the bricks and the slate;
then your cheek was wet
the way it gets
from the breeze off the surf
as you stroll by the sea.

There was nothing to keep you
from planning the walk,
the picnic, the footrace
you'd been training for.

One by one they left:
first pebbles and violets,
then white and gold weeds,
then the tall daffodils
and the taller azaleas,
then dogwoods, magnolias,
at the very end, oaks.

All that was left
was a circle of water,
a circle of blue,

the only other colors
the ones you'd picked up
and carried with you:
your clothes, your food,
the ones you used
to teach your children,
saying red, yellow,
grass, tree,
tulip.

April 2020

For the first eight weeks
I knew them only
by what my sister told me,
how the ducks appeared in the yard one day
acting as if they owned it, first the females,
then the males, her cat transfixed in fury,
standing upright against the window,
then the babies in a row, all this
a cheerful news report, a distraction,
how she set out a kiddy pool
and drove downtown to get them food,
getting into a routine, the parade
every morning, the afternoon retreat,
until I saw them too last week
as we sat in her driveway, carefully spaced,
visiting for the first time since it started;
the daddy ducks and one mom came out,
fat and waddling, red and white,
sniffing at my car, seeming dismayed
at something new and strange.
Yesterday in passing she said
that the fourteen were now six,
just as the neighbors had warned her,
that she could do nothing to save them,
had to look out each day and see
that more were gone.

Comet, 1986

When we went out to see Halley's Comet,
driving for miles and then walking,
we couldn't even make out the stars,
so we went to the all-night Kroger's
where we laughed at the tabloid headlines.

We still felt kind of wild,
being where no one would find us
when we should have been home asleep;
it made up for missing the comet,
and I knew that you and I both

were doing the math in our heads,
thinking that if we lived long enough
to be here when it returned,
we'd look at the sky some night,
wondering if we'd seen it,

remembering stepping over
a fence on somebody's farm,
fields of tobacco, dirt scuttling
under our comfortable sneakers—
and it didn't take many years

for most of us to be trespassing
in a future we don't belong to,
standing on a country road,
trying to look at the darkness
on the other side of the fence.

The Story of the Hurricane

We opened the front door after the storm
and stepped out into the neighborhood,
our shoes skidding and crunching
on a blanket of wet branches,
and when the porches and roofs
had been restored and the roads
cleared, we needed to share,
to compare our stories
repeatedly, the way we told
about the births of our children,
about the water breaking and the first pains,
the greens and the blues
of the ward's flowered wallpaper,
and how the snow wandered
and speckled the sky,
or the day of the flood, or the copperheads,
or the airplane we took
that turned and went back
to the airport, or the story
of the final illness, how he, how she,
exhaled that long decisive breath.

Witness

I ran into Nick on the library steps
after class, years ago,
and when he asked where I'd been,
I explained about the miscarriage.

What I remember is the look
he gave me when I said
that nothing that bad
had ever happened to me.

He looked at me,
but I knew he was seeing
something else, someone else,
and I was ashamed.

Today, taking a walk,
I thought of him,
almost wanting him to know
how things turned out,

but I know it's better
to leave him a witness
to something that pure,
to someone who lived

for a while, not knowing
that the first death is always
the first of many,
a beginning, not an end.

Visiting Your Father's Grave

It was somebody's idea
to drive out to the cemetery,
maybe a nephew, amped up on a memory

of cutting logs together for a neighbor,
your father smiling, handing him a beer,
so we all headed off in a dotted line,

the square of open land appearing
as if it had snuck up on us, popping out
like an unhappy jack-in-the-box.

We sat in our cars with the motors running,
savoring the heat until everyone arrived;
then we walked towards the grave,

getting lost for a while until we found it,
then taking pictures, smiling, until someone
thought it felt wrong. Then we frowned.

The plaque your sister put there years before,
setting it down beside the granite headstone,
had turned into a block of dull cement,

but she remembered being there that day,
finding it in the store and driving out,
deciding to write her name before she left

with Sharpie on one of the angel's wings;
how close she felt to him then,
the two of them alone together,

and how she thought she heard the angel singing
in a voice that was oddly familiar,
one she'd forgotten until that moment.

Nanook of the North

The Museum of the Moving Image, Queens, New York

We stand in a cluster
before the small screen
in silence, watching
a serious man
building an igloo,
one block at a time
in the falling snow.

His bundled children
mostly ignore him;
his wife is busy
with the baby and toddler;
he is there for us,
our eyes seem to meet,
then he turns to speak
to the cameraman.

He knows we will see him,
in some future time,
in some other place,
but we don't know
what was real, what was staged,
what he turned to say
to the woman near him
who was not his wife,
or if they laughed
at the three-sided igloo,
specially built
for the inside shots.

What we know instead
is that he was there,

building a home
like the one he lives in,
like the one he'll return to
with his own wife and children,
where he soon may sleep
under thick warm layers,
dreaming that the snow
he's shaped into blocks
is somehow still falling.

After the Storm

The army of chainsaws works all day,
and the sound overwhelms my house.

I stay inside; outside the window,
dozens of crows

dive-bomb the fig tree,
pecking at the mottled fruit.

So much that was hidden
is now in plain sight:

the lichen as green as a chrysalis,
the smooth leaves clinging

to splintered branches,
the acorns and the moss,

and the sudden memory
of *frais du bois*, tasting of bark,

a wildness in my mouth,
an opening of the world.

Music Lessons

College applications: my daughter's friend,
asked to write about "something you've lost,"
writes about his soprano voice,
which startles me, it seems so physical.

Everyone who hears this story stops,
considering how they'd answer,
each of them seeing an array
of faces getting older in a mirror.

What I think of is my flute, not lost,
but sitting in its thin case in my closet,
of carrying it with me into airports,
of holding it under my feet until we landed,

and of my uncle, booking a seat for his bass
every time the orchestra traveled,
how my cousins called it their sibling,
how they worried over finding it a home

after he died, even in their grief.
I think of how I practiced every day;
by now I'm sure the pads are torn or swollen.
Maybe twenty years ago

I took it out to see if I could play
and couldn't, remembering the fingering
but not the way to curve my hands enough
to cover up the keys with open holes.

It felt unnatural to hold my mouth
pursed like that, to hold my arms that high;
even that way of breathing's been erased,
has floated off like smoke or steam or air

or music dying at a vaulted ceiling.
Still, sometimes, when I hear that liquid sound,
it's like a memory of swimming naked
or knowing someone's body like my own,

someone who once sat and flew with me,
like my uncle's bass, memorialized
by my cousin's small tattoo,
something written on the skin.

Later Years: An Oar in the Sky

Alexa

She is ignorant and admits to being
easily confused.

She tells her jokes with a cheerfulness
that shows how lost she is.

I want to help her and teach her how
the world works,

and I love this feeling of knowing
so much more,

but it also makes me hate her
a little more each time,

each time she admits she's having trouble,
is helpless to assist,

like a mother of grown children,
who see her now

as someone who offers only facts
from the news,

a weather report, or a small repertoire
of songs and stories,

like the mother I may become,
sitting and nodding

as if I understood the talk,
chiming in

and coming to attention
when my name is spoken.

How it Starts

It starts when you enter a room
and your children are talking about you,
calling you "she," not "Mom."

For once, you hear them speaking
in their native tongue;
all this time they've been translating.

They hum melodies you've never heard
and mouth the lyrics, and their hands
form complicated patterns in the air.

It ends with them whispering
in a hallway, slowly circling
and then landing.

They come in and touch your arm
as if you are a bubble,
or a baby, or a flower.

Then they fly,
their small shadows flitting
from wall to wall to wall.

Near the End

Later someone told me
I had made the shift nurse cry.

For years, I thought this meant
that I was fierce.

I was fighting for my family,
I wasn't taking shit.

Only yesterday I wondered
if she'd simply pitied me

for taking the trouble to fight,
for thinking that things could change,

but then I decided no,
it wasn't that at all—

I just wanted to make my voice
into something jagged and sharp

and to slash somebody with it.

Zoom

One by one we notice
that she's frozen in that grimace
as we go on around her,
interrupting and flashing
our yellow outlines,
neatly stacked
like the blocks
of an artificial city;

once or twice we hear
staccato riffs
that mean nothing to us,
or she undergoes
a strange transformation,
this time blurring
into streaks and lines;

then for a long time,
nothing changes
in her little box;
and one of us says,
"I think we've lost her"—

impossible to tell
if she hears us or sees us,
if she's trying to speak,
or if she's truly gone.

Resting Bitch Face

The newspaper article says
that an RBF bar has opened:

no tipping or smiling required.
If I were to go,

I would have to be reborn
with yellow wings and claws,

pomegranate teeth, hair
made completely of scallions and diamonds,

I'd have to be miles high,
I'd have to be glass and lava,

I'd have to ooze through the walls,
rearranging everyone's atoms,

and even then, I might fail
to do more than the not tipping.

The Long-Distance Runner

I can't look away
from the smooth line he makes
as he curves and slaps
his way down the street,
a pedal, a piston,
a camel, sufficient,
an island of a man,
tapping out the rhythm
of a broken fan belt
on an Illinois highway,
a world of absolutes:
where you were, where you're going,
and corn to each side.
He flows into the pine woods,
flattening dry leaves,
and the weight of his body
is unbearable.

Ladybug

Is there anything more lost
than a February ladybug

crawling on the carpet
or anything more dead

than the dusty piles of them
that formed at the door

of our cabin in the mountains,
like the sand that forms hills

along weathered fence posts
four hundred miles away

where North Carolina
finally spills into the ocean,

where my children remember
that a waitress called me ladybug

at a hotel breakfast
where the milk was sour,

the cheery pattern
and the bright red shell

indicating nothing
of how dry, how light

they eventually become,
having flown so far

to reach their home
and find it in ashes.

Sky Diving

In the video that you sent,
she walks quickly with her teenage son
to the open door of the plane,
where they bump their fists together,
crouch down, and lean forward;
her arms stretch wide, and her hands
seem to scoop up and gather the sky.

She never would have guessed
what we know as we watch her plummet—
in a few years they'd both be gone,
and even the ground below them,
the trees and the brook, the hillside,
would be ploughed under and transformed,
would disappear from sight.

We watch her hair streaming back
like lines of migrating birds.
The instructor's arms circle her waist,
and someone is holding the camera.
She places her faith in these people,
who fall from morning to night,
witnessing every day

a landscape that never ends,
a sky that stretches forever.
She trusts them to keep her safe,
to protect her teenage son,
and believes them when they tell her
she has only to take that leap
and nothing will go wrong.

Jigsaw

Your mother tells me
how her own mother always talked
when she did jigsaw puzzles,

pushing the pieces in and muttering,
"I'll make you fit,"
under her breath.

I never met her,
but she feels like a friend;
I get just as mad

when things don't work.
It makes me smile
to think of her jabbing

stubbornly at the cardboard,
willing the knobs
to be smaller or different,

thinking that if the color's right,
the shape can't be wrong,
but even if she made it work,

she'd be left with a picture
full of ridges and rips,
an oar in the sky,

a seagull's wing
stabbing
its way into the sand.

On-ramp

When my mother stopped cold
at the end of the on-ramp,
it made sense—

the ramp was wide and open,
with a gentle curve
and a good view,

while what lay beyond it
was a sudden drench
of metal and heat,

and stopping
gave her time to think,
to plan a strategy

to get into those ribbons
smoothly, not causing
a buckle or a tear,

so she sat and watched,
suddenly noticing
the chocolate bar she'd brought

dripping on the dashboard,
and not the wave of cars
rising behind her.

Breathe In

My uncle's joke:
the man whose headphones tell him,
"Breathe in, breathe out,"
and when his girlfriend insists
that he take them off,
he dies. I thought it was funny;
my sister was horrified.

Young, we couldn't imagine
that our bodies might change.
Today, it's a song in the background
that I find myself moving to.
It's knowing there's something
over my shoulder, slipping away
when I turn to look.
It's an image
that won't come clear.

It's a notebook on the table,
waiting to be filled,
waiting to be color coded,
one message after the other.
It's my name appearing
on my clothing.

It's quiet now:
breathe in, breath out,
the timer chirps and the car flashes
orange warnings, then red,
and I walk without thinking
when the light turns green;
I rise from the table
like a marionette.

Not a Premonition but a Memory

That day you were coughing on the restaurant's porch,
I didn't think much of it.

I thought about it later, but that didn't count;
it was just another lunch, an avocado toast,

not a cliché, like the loud bird
pecking at the window near the chair

where the grandmother used to sit.
I wonder about that bird,

whether people believe that it hatched from the egg
already imbued with her spirit,

or if the spirit drifts from tree to tree
and finds the perfect bird to penetrate.

I'm wrong; it starts with memory
but turns into a pun,

one thing replacing another.
This happened in the dream I had

right after you told me your news:
you'd forgotten your name;

no matter what I said,
you kept insisting it was something else—

it took me a full day to think about that name
and realize what it meant.

The Dog Walkers

Like stars, they wheel in circles;
they rise and set with the sun.

Like birds, they congregate,
then fly their separate ways.

They see me and they don't;
I'm only a head and a wave,

but I can see them clearly:
how they work to adjust their pace,

how they wait without resentment
and look down patiently,

how they offer quiet words
as if in conversation,

meeting the demands
of bodies young and old,

tired or frenzied, sick
or not yet sick, not yet

needing to be cared for,
needing relief and food

and water set out, paws
carefully, gingerly washed.

The Next Generation

The hundred-year-old oaks that line the street
are finally dying off.

Of the forty or fifty I've known,
three or four remain.

One was hit by lightning
as I stood in my kitchen—

I jumped like a cat
and remembered years before

when my neighbor's tree was struck,
how I took my kids to see it,

the trunk smooth and white,
a carpet of bark on the grass.

We've all done our part, bought saplings
from the Public Works Department,

watered them, mulched them,
checked for buds each spring.

My other neighbor called her tree her "stick"—
I think of that whenever I pass by,

seeing it tall and full and thick,
wanting to stop and offer praise,

tell it how much it's grown,
as if it were the grandchild I don't have.

Instead I have these trees, these pioneers,
travelers who'll roll into the years

when someone else is living in this house,
wagon trains I glance at from my window

with pleasure and with interest, but
not loving them enough to truly care

whether they thrive or wither or decay.
It's better this way,

better the trees than children,
seeing them grow a little every year,

knowing there are always more to buy,
one tree very much like another,

none of them knowing who we were,
none of them reaching for my hand.

No Bicycles, No Golf Carts

It puzzles her, it worries her,
that wood-burned sign, those black
jaunty letters of instruction
at the foot of the small bridge
that spans the pond.

We rest in the splintered gazebo,
watching as she reads it, solves it,
reads it again, and then you stand
and push her chair out to a spot
where both of you can see the spray

made by the ducks who stand and flap
and see the backs of turtles, plums
floating in a dark green soup,
and everywhere the dragonflies,
like busy visitors from space,

but there it is on the other side,
persistent in its scolding,
as if we're guilty of some sin,
undeserving of even this much
small, harmless beauty.

Eclipse

Right after the eclipse, we all were crazy
to see another one, planning Cleveland
in seven years, Iceland in nine, hanging on
to that moment when the sun had disappeared,

leaving us stranded in the universe
with no control over our bodies,
which were pulled by the sight like puppets,
made to yell and point and cry,

but then we forgot it, went ahead
in our small predictable circles,
though for years I had remembered
an opioid, no longer in use,

that I'd tasted for ten minutes
when my first child was born,
had craved it and felt disappointed
when my second came too fast

for any drug at all,
had remembered that dreamy joy
after I'd erased everything else
about how labor felt, how I thought

oh yes, this as it started up again,
and how it disappeared,
eclipsed by the baby himself.
So little remains in my memory

of all those sleepless nights,
the heavy days that followed,

just pale scraps and slivers,
and when I sometimes try to hear again

the voices of the people that I've lost,
the longer that they're gone, the more I fail,
hearing instead their words in my own voice,
although I still retain the way I felt

hearing their voices then, like a vibration
continuing after the bell is stifled—
the obscure mathematics
of adding and subtracting pain and pleasure

leave me wondering what I'll recall
from any time of grief or time of joy,
looking now at the pictures we all took
of shimmering crescents underneath the trees,

the leaves transformed into a row of pinholes
that threw the alien sun down at our feet,
the most unearthly thing we'd ever seen
until we raised our faces to the sky.

Her Last Breath
for Randy Kafka

You imagine yourself,
seconds before she died,
making a different choice,

as if leaving the room
or turning your back
to adjust the TV's volume

could have made a difference.
Believe me when I tell you
it made no difference.

She was hardly in that place,
and you were a shadow
or a humming in her ears.

You could see the room,
the bed, the glare
of the harsh fluorescent lighting,

but all that she saw
was something singing
on the branch of a tree

that fluttered to her side,
landed on her arm,
and then retreated.

Homesick for Water

Homesick for water, though I can't claim it,
not being a boater, a fisher, a swimmer.
Homesick still for the sound of a river,
for crossing a bridge on the way to the store,
looking over the side, and for the canal,
for the snake of a trickle on undergrowth,
for interrupting tips of grass,
for the smell of clay on slimy banks,
for driftwood and small scuttling crabs,
for gray foam or the sky reflected,
for the air that voyages over it
and disembarks when we inhale,
homesick for plunging under,
or for being dry at a distance,
for changing into a floating creature,
for learning a new way to breathe,
for somewhere we've never been,
a place where we wash away.

About the Author

Ruth Bardon grew up in Highland Park, New Jersey, and lived in a number of midwestern cities before firmly settling in Durham, North Carolina. She received an MFA from the Iowa Writers Workshop in 1982 and a PhD in English from the University of North Carolina at Chapel Hill in 1995. Her poems have appeared in *The Southern Review, Boulevard, The Cincinnati Review, New Ohio Review, Salamander,* and other journals. She is the author of two chapbooks: *Demon Barber* (Main Street Rag, 2020) and *What You Wish For* (Finishing Line Press, 2023). She is also the author of *Selected Short Stories of William Dean Howells* (Ohio University Press, 1997).

Books are a way to explore, connect, and discover. Poetry incites us to observe and think in new ways, bridging our understanding of the world with our artistic need to interact with, shape, and share it with others.

Publishing poetry is our way of saying—

We love these words,
we want to preserve them,
we want to play a role in sharing them
with the world.

Follow Meadowlark Press
on Facebook & Instagram

facebook.com/ReadAMeadowlarkBook

@meadowlarkbooks

BIRDY POETRY PRIZE FINALISTS

2023
Five Reports of Fugitive Dust
Mary Mercier

"Here the reader is ushered into the natural world where so much is just waiting for us to uncover, to allow us to more readily 'glide into joy.' . . . Reading these poems filled me with a renewed sense of anticipation for the unnoticed and still-unrevealed wonder living all around us. I want to do as she says: 'Hold the shell that is the world. / Put it to your ear.'"

–Andrea Potos, *Her Joy Becomes* and *Marrow of Summer*

2022
No Matter How It Ends
E.J. Rode

"Thanks to E.J.'s masterful poetry, I'm less judgmental, think more deeply, and better understand our world and myself. If there were a position of Poet of Peace, and if I were in charge, I'd appoint E.J. With her literary wisdom, openness, and loving connection with humanity, there could be resolution to many of life's issues and personal problems."

–Jim Potter, *Deputy Jennings Meets the Amish*

2021
Lilac and Sawdust
Kenneth Pobo

"The two men at the center of this book (Jerry and Jeff) are both extraordinary and ordinary, and the poems chart their lives carefully, in great detail, with a loving gaze. The books lets us get to know them, as if they are dear friends, and the writing sparkles, written by someone with clear eyes, clear head, and a clear heart. This book will endear you to it too."

–Kevin Rabas, Poet Laureate of Kansas, 2017-2019, *More Than Words*

2020
Kansas Poems
Brian Daldorph

"Kansas Poems is a poetry of place and microhistory, which nonetheless transcends the people and events it tells about . . . And while I've never been to Kansas, I now feel that I might have—or at least that there is a Kansas of my mind, a place of lakes and fireflies and small lives."
—Laura Chalar, *Unlearning* and *Midnight at the Law Firm (Stories)*

2019
Valentine
Ruth Maus

"Wry and rue—it sounds like the recipe for a craft cocktail. But those are really the main ingredients in Ruth Maus's sly, wise, and expansive book . . . Most of her poems are short—and a lot bigger than they seem, poems marked by gallows, humor, and a poker face, and with just a twitch of a tell that reveals how much lies beneath their surface."
—Michael Gorra, *Portrait of a Novel: Henry and James and the making of an American Masterpiece*

Meadowlark Press created The Birdy Poetry Prize to celebrate the voices of our era. Cash prize, publication, and 50 complimentary copies awarded annually.

Accepting Entries: September 1 - December 1

Entry Fee: $25
Prize: $1,000 cash, publication by Meadowlark Press, 50 copies of the completed book

All entries will be considered for standard Meadowlark publishing contract offers, as well.

Full-length poetry manuscripts (55 page minimum) will be considered. Poems may be previously published in journals and/or anthologies, but not in full-length single-author volumes. Poets are eligible to enter, regardless of publishing history.

See meadowlarkbookstore.com for complete submission guidelines.